SexZ ABC'z

Nikita Beatty

authorHOUSE

AuthorHouse™
1663 Liberty Drive
Bloomington, IN 47403
www.authorhouse.com
Phone: 833-262-8899

Published by AuthorHouse 08/30/2022

ISBN: 978-1-6655-6862-3 (sc)
ISBN: 978-1-6655-6861-6 (e)

Print information available on the last page.

Any people depicted in stock imagery provided by Getty Images are models, and such images are being used for illustrative purposes only.
Certain stock imagery © Getty Images.

This book is printed on acid-free paper.

A nal

A ss

A nus

A

Annie the <u>Anus</u> anxiously awaited for Adam's aggressive <u>Anal</u> as she was an <u>Ass</u>.

B

reast

ooty

lowjob

B

Becky's bouncy <u>Breast</u> and bountiful <u>Booty</u> were nothing to her baffling <u>Blowjob</u>.

C

ock

lit

unt

C

Chris's <u>Cock</u> couldn't contain Candy's <u>Clit</u>, cause she was a classy <u>Cunt</u>.

Dick
Dildo
Doggy style

D

David's <u>Dick</u> didn't difference from a <u>Dildo</u> that's why Daisy digged <u>Doggy style.</u>

E

rection

rotic

jaculation

E

Erica's <u>Erotic</u> exercise engorged Erin's <u>Erection</u> for an explosive <u>Ejaculation</u>.

Foreplay
Fallacio
Finger-fucking

F

Fay-fay's <u>Foreplay</u> foreshadowed fascinating <u>Fallacio</u>, followed by frantic <u>Finger-fucking</u>.

Gagged

agged

uzzled

olden-shower

G

Grace <u>Gagged</u> and <u>Guzzled</u> gracefully as Greg gave her a glorious <u>Golden-shower.</u>

H orny
ard-on
ead

H

<u>Horny</u> hank has a horrible <u>Hard-on.</u>
Hopefully Hallie hurrys with the
<u>Head.</u>

I
mpotent

nches

ntimacy

I

Isaac's <u>Impotent</u> <u>Inches</u> ignited icy <u>Intimacy</u>.

J

ump-off

ack-off

izz

J

Jackie the <u>Jump-off</u> joyfully <u>Jacked-off</u> Jeff; jetting <u>Jizz</u> everywhere.

Kinky
Kissing
Kegels

K

Kathy's <u>Kinky</u> <u>Kissing</u> cause killer <u>Kegels</u>.

Licked
ube
ustfully

L

Lisa <u>Licked</u> the <u>Lube</u> <u>Lustfully</u> leaving Luke longing for more.

M otor-boated

oan

asturbated

M

Matt <u>Motor-boated</u> Mary making her <u>Moan</u>; while Misty moistly <u>Masturbated</u>.

N
aked
ipple
ut

N

Naked Nancy's Nipples need notorious amount of nutritious Nut.

O ral

rgy's

rgasm

O

Oliva observed overwhelming <u>Oral</u> <u>Orgy's</u>. Opening her orifices to optimal <u>Orgasms</u>.

Pussies

Penetrating

Penis

P

Paul's Pulsating <u>Penis</u> has <u>Penetrated</u> plenty of pretty <u>Pussies</u>.

Quickie
Queef
Quivering

Q

Q's quite <u>Quickie</u> caused Quita's quaking <u>Quivering</u> <u>Queefs</u>.

R agtime
ubbing
im-job

R

Rachel's <u>Ragtime</u> ruined Ryans's frisky <u>Rubbing</u>, resulting in a rigours <u>Rim-job</u>.

Spooned

quirt

alad-tossing

S

Steve <u>Spooned</u> Sasha slowly. Suddenly soft <u>Squirting</u> sprayed the surface. Setting up for a serious <u>Salad-tossing</u> situation.

T wat

itties

hreesome

T

Tiffany's tangy <u>Twat</u> and tantalizing <u>Titties</u> turned the two Tony's into a <u>Threesome</u>.

U

rine

nicorn

ncircumcised

U

Uncle Urkel's unique <u>Urine</u> <u>Unicorns</u> are usually <u>Uncircumcised</u>.

Voluptuous
Vagina
ibrator

V

Vicky's <u>Voluptuous</u> <u>Vagina</u> vigorously visited vast <u>Vibrators</u>.

W ang
ild
hoopie

W

William's <u>Wang</u> was willing ready for some <u>Wild</u> <u>Whoopie</u>.

X-rated

enerotica

X

Xavier exhibited <u>X-rated</u> <u>Xenerotica</u>.

Yummy
oni
earned

Y

Yavonne's <u>Yummy</u> <u>Yoni</u> <u>Yearned</u> for young men.

Z oophilla onked

Z

Zack's <u>Zoophilla</u> always left him <u>Zonked</u>.

Printed in the United States
by Baker & Taylor Publisher Services